The Must Make Macaroon Cookbook

More Amazing Macaroon Recipes

That You Could Ever Imagine!

Table of Contents

Introduction

Go preheat that oven, get out your mixing bowls and get ready to bake some of the best macaroons that you have ever had. These recipes are easy to make, full of flavor and are so creative that they will make you wonder how the flavor combinations ever came about. But don't worry about that, just enjoy the cookies and definitely give every single recipe a try.

I created this macaroon recipe book in order to share my love of macaroons with the world. I have played with various macaroon recipes for years, developing exciting and unique macaroons alongside more traditional flavored cookies. I also try to make each recipe as simple as possible, requiring no special equipment or crazy, rare ingredients. All of these macaroon recipes are accessible to everyone no matter where in the world you live or what your baking skill. If you can measure and stir, you can make a fantastic macaroon!

Now what to try first? The classic macaroon recipe of course! After you master that perfect cookie, you can move on to citrus macaroons or maybe double chocolate macaroons. What about cranberry macaroons or Nutella macaroons? Okay, maybe it is hard to decide where to begin! So open up this cookbook, close your eyes and point to a recipe- no matter where your finger lands, you will be making one of the best macaroons that you have ever had!

So what are you waiting for? Time to start making macaroons. That oven should be preheated and ready by now! Happy baking!

Classic Macaroon

If you love straightforward, amazing macaroons then this is the best recipe to try first. These cookies are chewy yet still have that great toasted coconut flavor that really makes macaroons irresistible.

Active Time: 15 minutes

Yield: 26 cookies

Ingredients

- 5 ½ cups coconut flakes, sweetened
- 1 tsp vanilla

- ¼ tsp salt
- 1 cup sweetened condensed milk
- 2 Tablespoons egg whites

Directions

1. In a little bowl, whisk the egg whites until stiff peaks form. Set aside

2. In a separate bowl, combine the remaining **Ingredients** and stir until well blended.

3. Fold in the whipped egg whites to the coconut mixture, folding gently so as not to knock the air out of the whipped whites.

4. Scoop the cookies onto a lined sheet tray using a tablespoon to measure the batter and form the scoop.

5. Bake in a preheated 325 F oven for 20 to 24 minutes or until the tops of the cookies are golden brown.

6. Let the cookies cool for 5-7 minutes then enjoy while warm or Store at the room temperature for up to one week.

Chocolate Dipped Macaroon

One of the easiest ways to make your macaroons go from boring to gourmet is to simply dip them in melted chocolate. This easy addition will make every bite even more amazing-you can't go wrong with coconut and chocolate!

Active Time: 15 minutes

Yield: 26 cookies

Ingredients

- 5 ½ cups coconut flakes, sweetened
- 1 tsp vanilla
- ¼ tsp salt

- 1 cup sweetened condensed milk
- 2 Tablespoons egg whites
- 1 cup mini chocolate chips

Directions

1. In a little bowl, whisk the egg whites until stiff peaks form. Set aside

2. In a separate bowl, combine the remaining **Ingredients** and stir until well blended.

3. Fold in the whipped egg whites to the coconut mixture, folding gently so as not to knock the air out of the whipped whites.

4. Scoop the cookies onto a lined sheet tray using a tablespoon to measure the batter and form the scoop.

5. Bake in a preheated 325F oven for 20 to 24 minutes or until the tops of the cookies are golden brown.

6. Let the cookies cool for about 5-6 minutes.

7. Melt the chocolate chips over a double boiler, stirring constantly so that the chocolate doesn't burn.

8. Dip the bottoms of the macaroons into the chocolate, letting the chocolate go about ½ way up the cookie. Let the chocolate drip off the cookie for a few seconds then place the cookie on a sheet tray.

9. Store at the room temperature for up to one week.

Cranberry Macaroons

Sweet and tart dried cranberries are always the perfect compliment to coconut macaroons. The chewy texture of the cranberries goes well with the chewiness of the cookies making it a seamless combination.

Active Time: 15 minutes

Yield: 26 cookies

Ingredients

- 5 ½ cups coconut flakes, sweetened
- 1 tsp vanilla
- ¼ tsp salt
- 1 cup sweetened condensed milk
- 2 Tablespoons egg whites
- 1 cup dried cranberries

Directions

1. In a little bowl, whisk the egg whites until stiff peaks form. Set aside

2. In a separate bowl, combine the remaining **Ingredients** and stir until well blended.

3. Fold in the whipped egg whites to the coconut mixture, folding gently so as not to knock the air out of the whipped whites.

4. Scoop the cookies onto a lined sheet tray using a tablespoon to measure the batter and form the scoop.

5. Bake in a preheated 325F oven for 20 to 24 minutes or until the tops of the cookies are golden brown.

6. Let the cookies cool for about 5-6 minutes then enjoy while warm or Store at the room temperature for up to one week.

Chocolate Chip Macaroons

While it is standard to have chocolate on the outside of coconut macaroons, wouldn't it be great to have chocolate inside too? When the chocolate chips are baked into the cookie, they become deliciously melted and taste amazing in this great cookie.

Active Time: 15 minutes

Yield: 26 cookies

Ingredients

- 5 ½ cups coconut flakes, sweetened
- 1 tsp vanilla
- ¼ tsp salt
- 1 cup sweetened condensed milk
- 2 Tablespoons egg whites
- 1 cup chocolate chips

Directions

1. In a little bowl, whisk the egg whites until stiff peaks form. Set aside

2. In a separate bowl, combine the remaining **Ingredients** and stir until well blended.

3. Fold in the whipped egg whites to the coconut mixture, folding gently so as not to knock the air out of the whipped whites.

4. Scoop the cookies onto a lined sheet tray using a tablespoon to measure the batter and form the scoop.

5. Bake in a preheated 325F oven for 20 to 24 minutes or until the tops of the cookies are golden brown.

6. Let the cookies cool for about 5-6 minutes then enjoy while warm or Store at the room temperature for up to one week.

Cherry Macaroons

Cherry and coconut is a great combination that you are sure to enjoy. Dried cherries are a fantastic way to add flavor and texture to these classic cookies.

Active Time: 15 minutes

Yield: 26 cookies

Ingredients

- 5 ½ cups coconut flakes, sweetened
- 1 tsp vanilla
- ¼ tsp salt

- 1 cup sweetened condensed milk
- 2 Tablespoons egg whites
- 1 cup dried cherries, chopped

Directions

1. In a little bowl, whisk the egg whites until stiff peaks form. Set aside

2. In a separate bowl, combine the remaining **Ingredients** and stir until well blended.

3. Fold in the whipped egg whites to the coconut mixture, folding gently so as not to knock the air out of the whipped whites.

4. Scoop the cookies onto a lined sheet tray using a tablespoon to measure the batter and form the scoop.

5. Bake in a preheated 325F oven for 20 to 24 minutes or until the tops of the cookies are golden brown.

6. Let the cookies cool for about 5-6 minutes then enjoy while warm or Store at the room temperature for up to one week.

Caramel Macaroons

While these macaroons may look normal to the eye, one bite will find that they are extraordinary. Sweet and rich, just one of these cookies will be enough to satisfy any sweet tooth.

Active Time: 15 minutes

Yield: 26 cookies

Ingredients

- 5 ½ cups coconut flakes, sweetened
- 1 tsp vanilla

- ¼ tsp salt
- 3/4 cup sweetened condensed milk
- ¼ cup caramel sauce
- 2 Tablespoons egg whites

Directions

1. In a little bowl, whisk the egg whites until stiff peaks form. Set aside

2. In a separate bowl, combine the remaining **Ingredients** and stir until well blended.

3. Fold in the whipped egg whites to the coconut mixture, folding gently so as not to knock the air out of the whipped whites.

4. Scoop the cookies onto a lined sheet tray using a tablespoon to measure the batter and form the scoop.

5. Bake in a preheated 325F oven for 20 to 24 minutes or until the tops of the cookies are golden brown.

6. Let the cookies cool for about 5-6 minutes then enjoy while warm or Store at the room temperature for up to one week.

Almond Macaroon

Almond macaroons are one of those cookies that is easy to make but is something everyone will crave. After taking one bite, your taste buds will be dancing with the delicious almond flavor that is a fun surprise in these cookies.

Active Time: 15 minutes

Yield: 26 cookies

Ingredients

- 5 ½ cups coconut flakes, sweetened
- ¼ tsp salt
- 1 cup sweetened condensed milk
- 2 Tablespoons egg whites
- 1 tsp almond extract

Directions

1. In a little bowl, whisk the egg whites until stiff peaks form. Set aside

2. In a separate bowl, combine the remaining **Ingredients** and stir until well blended.

3. Fold in the whipped egg whites to the coconut mixture, folding gently so as not to knock the air out of the whipped whites.

4. Scoop the cookies onto a lined sheet tray using a tablespoon to measure the batter and form the scoop.

5. Bake in a preheated 325F oven for 20 to 24 minutes or until the tops of the cookies are golden brown.

6. Let the cookies cool for about 5-6 minutes then enjoy while warm or Store at the room temperature for up to one week.

Almond Crunch Macaroons

While most macaroons are chewy all the way through, it is a nice switch to have a crunchy texture inside the cookie. The addition of almonds helps make a regular macaroon more exciting and tantalizing. This is a macaroon recipe you're sure to love!

Active Time: 15 minutes

Yield: 26 cookies

Ingredients

- 5 ½ cups coconut flakes, sweetened
- 1 tsp almond extract
- 1 cup sweetened condensed milk
- 2 Tablespoons egg whites
- ¼ tsp salt
- 1 cup sliced almonds

Directions

1. In a little bowl, whisk the egg whites until stiff peaks form. Set aside

2. In a separate bowl, combine the remaining **Ingredients** and stir until well blended.

3. Fold in the whipped egg whites to the coconut mixture, folding gently so as not to knock the air out of the whipped whites.

4. Scoop the cookies onto a lined sheet tray using a tablespoon to measure the batter and form the scoop.

5. Bake in a preheated 325F oven for 20 to 24 minutes or until the tops of the cookies are golden brown.

6. Let the cookies cool for about 5-6 minutes then enjoy while warm or Store at the room temperature for up to one week.

Pineapple Macaroons

What an amazing, tropical cookie! Eating one of these delicious treats will make you feel as though you are sitting on a tropical island, relaxing with a yummy cookie that exudes flavor.

Active Time: 15 minutes

Yield: 26 cookies

Ingredients

- 5 ½ cups coconut flakes, sweetened
- 1 tsp vanilla
- ¼ tsp salt
- 1 cup sweetened condensed milk
- 2 Tablespoons egg whites
- 1 cup chopped, dried pineapple

Directions

1. In a little bowl, whisk the egg whites until stiff peaks form. Set aside

2. In a separate bowl, combine the remaining **Ingredients** and stir until well blended.

3. Fold in the whipped egg whites to the coconut mixture, folding gently so as not to knock the air out of the whipped whites.

4. Scoop the cookies onto a lined sheet tray using a tablespoon to measure the batter and form the scoop.

5. Bake in a preheated 325F oven for 20 to 24 minutes or until the tops of the cookies are golden brown.

6. Let the cookies cool for about 5-6 minutes then enjoy while warm or Store at the room temperature for up to one week.

Espresso Macaroon

Coffee and coconut may not be a combination you see often but once you give it a try, you will be a true believer in this blend. A touch of espresso powder goes a long way in this recipe and adds lots of flavor.

Active Time: 15 minutes

Yield: 26 cookies

Ingredients

- 5 ½ cups coconut flakes, sweetened
- 1 tsp vanilla
- ¼ tsp salt
- 1 cup sweetened condensed milk
- 2 Tablespoons Instant espresso powder
- 2 Tablespoons egg whites

Directions

1. In a little bowl, whisk the egg whites until stiff peaks form. Set aside

2. In a separate bowl, combine the remaining **Ingredients** and stir until well blended.

3. Fold in the whipped egg whites to the coconut mixture, folding gently so as not to knock the air out of the whipped whites.

4. Scoop the cookies onto a lined sheet tray using a tablespoon to measure the batter and form the scoop.

5. Bake in a preheated 325F oven for 20 to 24 minutes or until the tops of the cookies are golden brown.

6. Let the cookies cool for about 5-6 minutes then enjoy while warm or Store at the room temperature for up to one week.

Mocha Macaroons

Chocolate, espresso and coconut all blends together to make a cookie that is unforgettable. Make extra of these cookies whenever you bake as everyone will be asking for them!

Active Time: 15 minutes

Yield: 26 cookies

Ingredients

- 5 ½ cups coconut flakes, sweetened
- 1 tsp vanilla

- ¼ tsp salt
- 1 cup sweetened condensed milk
- ¼ cup cocoa powder, unsweetened
- 1 Tablespoon instant espresso powder
- 2 Tablespoons egg whites

Directions

1. In a little bowl, whisk the egg whites until stiff peaks form. Set aside

2. In a separate bowl, combine the remaining **Ingredients** and stir until well blended.

3. Fold in the whipped egg whites to the coconut mixture, folding gently so as not to knock the air out of the whipped whites.

4. Scoop the cookies onto a lined sheet tray using a tablespoon to measure the batter and form the scoop.

5. Bake in a preheated 325F oven for 20 to 24 minutes or until the tops of the cookies are golden brown.

6. Let the cookies cool for about 5-6 minutes then enjoy while warm or Store at the room temperature for up to one week.

Raspberry Macaroons

Rich, sweet raspberry jam is blended into these cookies making a dessert that is not only incredibly tasty but also beautiful. These cookies will be a pretty pink color even after they bake!

Active Time: 15 minutes

Yield: 26 cookies

Ingredients

- 5 ½ cups coconut flakes, sweetened
- ¼ cup raspberry jam

- ½ tsp vanilla extract
- ¼ tsp salt
- ¾ cup sweetened condensed milk
- 2 Tablespoons egg whites

Directions

1. In a little bowl, whisk the egg whites until stiff peaks form. Set aside

2. In a separate bowl, combine the remaining **Ingredients** and stir until well blended.

3. Fold in the whipped egg whites to the coconut mixture, folding gently so as not to knock the air out of the whipped whites.

4. Scoop the cookies onto a lined sheet tray using a tablespoon to measure the batter and form the scoop.

5. Bake in a preheated 325F oven for 20 to 24 minutes or until the tops of the cookies are golden brown.

6. Let the cookies cool for about 5-6 minutes then enjoy while warm or Store at the room temperature for up to one week.

Lemon Macaroons

A subtle lemon flavor makes a coconut macaroon go from basic to fantastic. Enjoy these refreshing cookies in the summertime when a lemon flavored treat is exactly what you need to cool you down.

Active Time: 15 minutes

Yield: 26 cookies

Ingredients

- 5 ½ cups coconut flakes, sweetened
- ½ tsp lemon extract
- 1 tsp lemon zest
- ¼ tsp salt
- 1 cup sweetened condensed milk
- 2 Tablespoons egg whites

Directions

1. In a little bowl, whisk the egg whites until stiff peaks form. Set aside

2. In a separate bowl, combine the remaining **Ingredients** and stir until well blended.

3. Fold in the whipped egg whites to the coconut mixture, folding gently so as not to knock the air out of the whipped whites.

4. Scoop the cookies onto a lined sheet tray using a tablespoon to measure the batter and form the scoop.

5. Bake in a preheated 325F oven for 20 to 24 minutes or until the tops of the cookies are golden brown.

6. Let the cookies cool for about 5-6 minutes then enjoy while warm or Store at the room temperature for up to one week.

Butterscotch Macaroon

There is something magical about the combination of butterscotch and coconut. Be careful when making these cookies because they are addictive- you'll need to make them all the time!

Active Time: 15 minutes

Yield: 30 cookies

Ingredients

- 5 ½ cups coconut flakes, sweetened
- 1 tsp vanilla
- ¼ tsp salt
- 1 cup sweetened condensed milk
- 2 Tablespoons egg whites
- 1 cup butterscotch chips

Directions

1. In a little bowl, whisk the egg whites until stiff peaks form. Set aside

2. In a separate bowl, combine the remaining **Ingredients** and stir until well blended.

3. Fold in the whipped egg whites to the coconut mixture, folding gently so as not to knock the air out of the whipped whites.

4. Scoop the cookies onto a lined sheet tray using a tablespoon to measure the batter and form the scoop.

5. Bake in a preheated 325F oven for 20 to 24 minutes or until the tops of the cookies are golden brown.

6. Let the cookies cool for about 5-6 minutes then enjoy while warm or Store at the room temperature for up to one week.

Double Chocolate Macaroon

Do you love chocolate? Do you want some extra chocolate with your cookies? This is the recipe for you! These macaroons are loaded with chocolate and will quickly become one of your go to chocolate desserts.

Active Time: 15 minutes

Yield: 26 cookies

Ingredients

- 5 ½ cups coconut flakes, sweetened
- 1 tsp vanilla
- ¼ tsp salt
- 1 cup sweetened condensed milk
- ¼ cup unsweetened cocoa powder
- 2 Tablespoons egg whites
- 1 cup mini chocolate chips

Directions

1. In a little bowl, whisk the egg whites until stiff peaks form. Set aside

2. In a separate bowl, combine the remaining **Ingredients** and stir until well blended.

3. Fold in the whipped egg whites to the coconut mixture, folding gently so as not to knock the air out of the whipped whites.

4. Scoop the cookies onto a lined sheet tray using a tablespoon to measure the batter and form the scoop.

5. Bake in a preheated 325F oven for 20 to 24 minutes or until the tops of the cookies are golden brown.

6. Let the cookies cool for about 5-6 minutes.

7. Melt the chocolate chips over a double boiler, stirring constantly so that the chocolate doesn't burn.

8. Dip the bottoms of the macaroons into the chocolate, letting the chocolate go about ½ way up the cookie. Let the chocolate drip off the cookie for a few seconds then place the cookie on a sheet tray.

9. Store at the room temperature for up to one week.

Honey Macaroons

Honey is a great way to give your macaroons a little something special without wavering from the traditional cookie. The rich flavor of honey is a great compliment to this little chewy treat.

Active Time: 15 minutes

Yield: 26 cookies

Ingredients

- 5 ½ cups coconut flakes, sweetened
- 1 tsp vanilla

- ¼ tsp salt
- ¾ cup sweetened condensed milk
- ¼ cup honey
- 2 Tablespoons egg whites

Directions

1. In a little bowl, whisk the egg whites until stiff peaks form. Set aside

2. In a separate bowl, combine the remaining **Ingredients** and stir until well blended.

3. Fold in the whipped egg whites to the coconut mixture, folding gently so as not to knock the air out of the whipped whites.

4. Scoop the cookies onto a lined sheet tray using a tablespoon to measure the batter and form the scoop.

5. Bake in a preheated 325F oven for 20 to 24 minutes or until the tops of the cookies are golden brown.

6. Let the cookies cool for about 5-6 minutes then enjoy while warm or Store at the room temperature for up to one week.

Orange Chocolate Macaroon

Orange and chocolate are two flavors that go well with almost anything. Now, that classic combo comes together in these chewy, flavorful cookies that are perfect for any time of year.

Active Time: 15 minutes

Yield: 26 cookies

Ingredients

- 5 ½ cups coconut flakes, sweetened
- 1 Tablespoon orange juice

- ¼ tsp salt
- 1 Tablespoon orange zest
- 1 cup sweetened condensed milk
- 2 Tablespoons egg whites
- 1 cup mini chocolate chips

Directions

1. In a little bowl, whisk the egg whites until stiff peaks form. Set aside

2. In a separate bowl, combine the remaining **Ingredients** and stir until well blended.

3. Fold in the whipped egg whites to the coconut mixture, folding gently so as not to knock the air out of the whipped whites.

4. Scoop the cookies onto a lined sheet tray using a tablespoon to measure the batter and form the scoop.

5. Bake in a preheated 325F oven for 20 to 24 minutes or until the tops of the cookies are golden brown.

6. Let the cookies cool for about 5-6 minutes.

7. Melt the chocolate chips over a double boiler, stirring constantly so that the chocolate doesn't burn.

8. Dip the bottoms of the macaroons into the chocolate, letting the chocolate go about ½ way up the cookie. Let the chocolate drip off the cookie for a few seconds then place the cookie on a sheet tray.

9. Store at the room temperature for up to one week.

Citrus Macaroon

If a bright and refreshing cookie is what you want, give this recipe a try. The zest from the citrus fruits lightens up the cookie, making it taste less sweet and more tangy.

Active Time: 15 minutes

Yield: 26 cookies

Ingredients

- 5 ½ cups coconut flakes, sweetened
- 1 tsp vanilla
- ¼ tsp salt
- 1 tsp lemon zest
- ½ tsp lime zest
- ½ tsp orange zest
- 1 cup sweetened condensed milk
- 2 Tablespoons egg whites

Directions

1. In a little bowl, whisk the egg whites until stiff peaks form. Set aside

2. In a separate bowl, combine the remaining **Ingredients** and stir until well blended.

3. Fold in the whipped egg whites to the coconut mixture, folding gently so as not to knock the air out of the whipped whites.

4. Scoop the cookies onto a lined sheet tray using a tablespoon to measure the batter and form the scoop.

5. Bake in a preheated 325F oven for 20 to 24 minutes or until the tops of the cookies are golden brown.

6. Let the cookies cool for about 5-6 minutes then enjoy while warm or Store at the room temperature for up to one week.

Spiced Macaroons

While you may think coconut macaroons are a summery dessert, this recipe will convince you that they are great for fall. A few simple spices make a cookie that is great for any fall or winter party or just to snack on at home.

Active Time: 15 minutes

Yield: 26 cookies

Ingredients

- 5 ½ cups coconut flakes, sweetened
- 1 tsp vanilla

- ¼ tsp salt
- ½ tsp cinnamon
- ¼ tsp nutmeg
- ¼ tsp ground ginger
- 1 cup sweetened condensed milk
- 2 Tablespoons egg whites

Directions

1. In a little bowl, whisk the egg whites until stiff peaks form. Set aside

2. In a separate bowl, combine the remaining **Ingredients** and stir until well blended.

3. Fold in the whipped egg whites to the coconut mixture, folding gently so as not to knock the air out of the whipped whites.

4. Scoop the cookies onto a lined sheet tray using a tablespoon to measure the batter and form the scoop.

5. Bake in a preheated 325F oven for 20 to 24 minutes or until the tops of the cookies are golden brown.

6. Let the cookies cool for about 5-6 minutes then enjoy while warm or Store at the room temperature for up to one week.

Ginger Macaroons

Fresh ginger shines in this cookie. Peel the ginger well before you grate it into the cookie batter and use the peels to add flavor to some water. Double ginger treats!

Active Time: 15 minutes

Yield: 26 cookies

Ingredients

- 5 ½ cups coconut flakes, sweetened
- 1 tsp vanilla
- ¼ tsp salt

- 1 ½ tsp fresh grated ginger
- 1 cup sweetened condensed milk
- 2 Tablespoons egg whites

Directions

1. In a little bowl, whisk the egg whites until stiff peaks form. Set aside

2. In a separate bowl, combine the remaining **Ingredients** and stir until well blended.

3. Fold in the whipped egg whites to the coconut mixture, folding gently so as not to knock the air out of the whipped whites.

4. Scoop the cookies onto a lined sheet tray using a tablespoon to measure the batter and form the scoop.

5. Bake in a preheated 325F oven for 20 to 24 minutes or until the tops of the cookies are golden brown.

6. Let the cookies cool for about 5-6 minutes then enjoy while warm or Store at the room temperature for up to one week.

Turmeric Macaroons

Turmeric has numerous health benefits, such as fighting inflammation, in addition to the fact that it is extremely flavorful and exotic. These cookies will not only be delicious but can also help you get on the right track health wise!

Active Time: 15 minutes

Yield: 26 cookies

Ingredients

- 5 ½ cups coconut flakes, sweetened
- 1 tsp vanilla

- ¼ tsp salt
- 1 tsp ground turmeric
- 1 cup sweetened condensed milk
- 2 Tablespoons egg whites

Directions

1. In a little bowl, whisk the egg whites until stiff peaks form. Set aside

2. In a separate bowl, combine the remaining **Ingredients** and stir until well blended.

3. Fold in the whipped egg whites to the coconut mixture, folding gently so as not to knock the air out of the whipped whites.

4. Scoop the cookies onto a lined sheet tray using a tablespoon to measure the batter and form the scoop.

5. Bake in a preheated 325F oven for 20 to 24 minutes or until the tops of the cookies are golden brown.

6. Let the cookies cool for about 5-6 minutes then enjoy while warm or Store at the room temperature for up to one week.

Vanilla Bean Macaroon

The job of vanilla beans inside macaroons is two fold. First, the vanilla beans add tons of flavor. Second, they are simply beautiful, making the cookies picture perfect!

Active Time: 15 minutes

Yield: 26 cookies

Ingredients

- 5 ½ cups coconut flakes, sweetened
- 1 Tablespoon vanilla bean paste

- ¼ tsp salt
- 1 cup sweetened condensed milk
- 2 Tablespoons egg whites

Directions

1. In a little bowl, whisk the egg whites until stiff peaks form. Set aside

2. In a separate bowl, combine the remaining **Ingredients** and stir until well blended.

3. Fold in the whipped egg whites to the coconut mixture, folding gently so as not to knock the air out of the whipped whites.

4. Scoop the cookies onto a lined sheet tray using a tablespoon to measure the batter and form the scoop.

5. Bake in a preheated 325F oven for 20 to 24 minutes or until the tops of the cookies are golden brown.

6. Let the cookies cool for about 5-6 minutes then enjoy while warm or Store at the room temperature for up to one week.

Curry Macaroons

If you are interested in making a super interesting macaroon cookie, start here. The sweet and savory taste combination will be sure to delight and excite you!

Active Time: 15 minutes

Yield: 26 cookies

Ingredients

- 5 ½ cups coconut flakes, sweetened
- 1 ½ tsp curry powder
- ¼ tsp salt

- 1 cup sweetened condensed milk
- 2 Tablespoons egg whites

Directions

1. In a little bowl, whisk the egg whites until stiff peaks form. Set aside

2. In a separate bowl, combine the remaining **Ingredients** and stir until well blended.

3. Fold in the whipped egg whites to the coconut mixture, folding gently so as not to knock the air out of the whipped whites.

4. Scoop the cookies onto a lined sheet tray using a tablespoon to measure the batter and form the scoop.

5. Bake in a preheated 325F oven for 20 to 24 minutes or until the tops of the cookies are golden brown.

6. Let the cookies cool for about 5-6 minutes then enjoy while warm or Store at the room temperature for up to one week.

Coconut Cardamom Macaroon

Spices can make a world of difference when added into a cookie. While you may not think of cardamom as being a dessert spice, when you pair it with coconut, it definitely is!

Active Time: 15 minutes

Yield: 26 cookies

Ingredients

- 5 ½ cups coconut flakes, sweetened
- 1 tsp vanilla
- ¼ tsp salt

- 1 tsp ground cardamom
- 1 cup sweetened condensed milk
- 2 Tablespoons egg whites

Directions

1. In a little bowl, whisk the egg whites until stiff peaks form. Set aside

2. In a separate bowl, combine the remaining **Ingredients** and stir until well blended.

3. Fold in the whipped egg whites to the coconut mixture, folding gently so as not to knock the air out of the whipped whites.

4. Scoop the cookies onto a lined sheet tray using a tablespoon to measure the batter and form the scoop.

5. Bake in a preheated 325F oven for 20 to 24 minutes or until the tops of the cookies are golden brown.

6. Let the cookies cool for about 5-6 minutes then enjoy while warm or Store at the room temperature for up to one week.

Lime Macaroons

Fresh and zesty, bright and sweet, this is a macaroon recipe to keep forever. Enjoy these macaroons in the summertime, or any time! Coconut and lime is always in season.

Active Time: 15 minutes

Yield: 26 cookies

Ingredients

- 5 ½ cups coconut flakes, sweetened
- 1 tsp vanilla
- ¼ tsp salt
- 2 Tablespoons key lime juice
- 1 Tablespoon lime zest
- 1 cup sweetened condensed milk
- 2 Tablespoons egg whites

Directions

1. In a little bowl, whisk the egg whites until stiff peaks form. Set aside

2. In a separate bowl, combine the remaining **Ingredients** and stir until well blended.

3. Fold in the whipped egg whites to the coconut mixture, folding gently so as not to knock the air out of the whipped whites.

4. Scoop the cookies onto a lined sheet tray using a tablespoon to measure the batter and form the scoop.

5. Bake in a preheated 325F oven for 20 to 24 minutes or until the tops of the cookies are golden brown.

6. Let the cookies cool for about 5-6 minutes then enjoy while warm or Store at the room temperature for up to one week.

Strawberry Macaroon

Strawberries and coconut are always a win. Using strawberry jam to add strawberry flavor is an easy way to make an amazing cookie.

Active Time: 15 minutes

Yield: 26 cookies

Ingredients

- 5 ½ cups coconut flakes, sweetened
- 1 tsp vanilla
- ¼ tsp salt
- ¾ cup sweetened condensed milk
- 2 Tablespoons egg whites
- ½ cup strawberry jam

Directions

1. In a little bowl, whisk the egg whites until stiff peaks form. Set aside

2. In a separate bowl, combine the remaining **Ingredients** and stir until well blended.

3. Fold in the whipped egg whites to the coconut mixture, folding gently so as not to knock the air out of the whipped whites.

4. Scoop the cookies onto a lined sheet tray using a tablespoon to measure the batter and form the scoop.

5. Bake in a preheated 325F oven for 20 to 24 minutes or until the tops of the cookies are golden brown.

6. Let the cookies cool for about 5-6 minutes then enjoy while warm or Store at the room temperature for up to one week.

Hazelnut Macaroons

Hazelnuts not only add a tasty crunch to these macaroons but the rich taste is something that is crave worthy. Hazelnuts and coconut? How could you say no to that?!

Active Time: 15 minutes

Yield: 26 cookies

Ingredients

- 5 ½ cups coconut flakes, sweetened
- 1 tsp vanilla
- ¼ tsp salt
- 1 cup sweetened condensed milk
- 1 cup chopped hazelnuts
- 2 Tablespoons egg whites

Directions

1. In a little bowl, whisk the egg whites until stiff peaks form. Set aside

2. In a separate bowl, combine the remaining **Ingredients** and stir until well blended.

3. Fold in the whipped egg whites to the coconut mixture, folding gently so as not to knock the air out of the whipped whites.

4. Scoop the cookies onto a lined sheet tray using a tablespoon to measure the batter and form the scoop.

5. Bake in a preheated 325F oven for 20 to 24 minutes or until the tops of the cookies are golden brown.

6. Let the cookies cool for about 5-6 minutes then enjoy while warm or Store at the room temperature for up to one week.

Nutella Macaroons

Everyone loves Nutella and everyone loves macaroons so this recipe was just meant to be! Smooth chocolate, hazelnut spread is a perfect blend to the sweet coconut inside macaroons.

Active Time: 15 minutes

Yield: 26 cookies

Ingredients

- 5 ½ cups coconut flakes, sweetened
- 1 tsp vanilla
- ¼ tsp salt
- ¾ cup sweetened condensed milk

- ¼ nutella, softened
- 2 Tablespoons egg whites

Directions

1. In a little bowl, whisk the egg whites until stiff peaks form. Set aside

2. In a separate bowl, combine the
remaining **Ingredients** and stir until well blended.

3. Fold in the whipped egg whites to the coconut mixture, folding gently so as not to knock the air out of the whipped whites.

4. Scoop the cookies onto a lined sheet tray using a tablespoon to measure the batter and form the scoop.

5. Bake in a preheated 325F oven for 20 to 24 minutes or until the tops of the cookies are golden brown.

6. Let the cookies cool for about 5-6 minutes then enjoy while warm or Store at the room temperature for up to one week.

Lemongrass Macaroon

While macarons are usually considered a dessert, you could definitely serve these cookies as an appetizer. The savory taste of the lemongrass makes this a versatile and tasty treat.

Active Time: 15 minutes

Yield: 26 cookies

Ingredients

- 5 ½ cups coconut flakes, sweetened
- 1 tsp vanilla
- ¼ tsp salt
- 2 Tablespoons chopped lemongrass
- 1 cup sweetened condensed milk
- 2 Tablespoons egg whites

Directions

1. In a little bowl, whisk the egg whites until stiff peaks form. Set aside

2. In a separate bowl, combine the remaining **Ingredients** and stir until well blended.

3. Fold in the whipped egg whites to the coconut mixture, folding gently so as not to knock the air out of the whipped whites.

4. Scoop the cookies onto a lined sheet tray using a tablespoon to measure the batter and form the scoop.

5. Bake in a preheated 325F oven for 20 to 24 minutes or until the tops of the cookies are golden brown.

6. Let the cookies cool for about 5-6 minutes then enjoy while warm or Store at the room temperature for up to one week.

Mango Macaroons

Coconut is a true tropical fruit which means it pairs well with all other tropical fruits. Chewy dried mango and toasted coconut? It's a natural fit!

Active Time: 15 minutes

Yield: 26 cookies

Ingredients

- 5 ½ cups coconut flakes, sweetened
- 1 tsp vanilla
- ¼ tsp salt
- 1 cup sweetened condensed milk

- 2 Tablespoons egg whites
- 1 cup chopped dried mango

Directions

1. In a little bowl, whisk the egg whites until stiff peaks form. Set aside

2. In a separate bowl, combine the remaining **Ingredients** and stir until well blended.

3. Fold in the whipped egg whites to the coconut mixture, folding gently so as not to knock the air out of the whipped whites.

4. Scoop the cookies onto a lined sheet tray using a tablespoon to measure the batter and form the scoop.

5. Bake in a preheated 325F oven for 20 to 24 minutes or until the tops of the cookies are golden brown.

6. Let the cookies cool for about 5-6 minutes then enjoy while warm or Store at the room temperature for up to one week.

Banana Macaroons

These cookies taste as if you combined banana bread with macaroons- sounds pretty great, right?! Opt for the ripest bananas you can find as they have the most flavor.

Active Time: 15 minutes

Yield: 26 cookies

Ingredients

- 5 ½ cups coconut flakes, sweetened
- 1 tsp vanilla
- 1 tsp cinnamon

- 1 banana, mashed
- ¼ tsp salt
- ½ cup sweetened condensed milk
- 2 Tablespoons egg whites

Directions

1. In a little bowl, whisk the egg whites until stiff peaks form. Set aside

2. In a separate bowl, combine the remaining **Ingredients** and stir until well blended.

3. Fold in the whipped egg whites to the coconut mixture, folding gently so as not to knock the air out of the whipped whites.

4. Scoop the cookies onto a lined sheet tray using a tablespoon to measure the batter and form the scoop.

5. Bake in a preheated 325F oven for 20 to 24 minutes or until the tops of the cookies are golden brown.

6. Let the cookies cool for about 5-6 minutes then enjoy while warm or Store at the room temperature for up to one week.

Made in the USA
Monee, IL
10 February 2023

27463803R00048